The Executive's Guide To:
Successfully Commissioning Video Productions

The Executive's Guide To:
Successfully Commissioning Video Productions

James Rostance

The Executive's Guide To:
Successfully Commissioning Video Productions

© 2015 Michael Lawson Publishing
Publish Date 28th April 2015
All right reserved

ISBN: 0956435424
ISBN-13: 978-0-956435422

This Book Is Dedicated To:

John Allen, lifetime experienced film and video producer whose professional teachings and influence as a true English gentleman is something I will always be thankful for.

Andy Longstaff, BBC cameraman and Senior Technical Operator, for taking me under his wing and teaching me his craft. I forget how many times he got me with the hot teaspoon gag, but his ability to make shoots fun whilst producing first class work is something that will always remain with me.

My parents, still the best I've ever had. And a particular thank you for buying the family video camera, which in 1992 was quite something. Apologies for editing all subsequent family videos with rave music, at the time it seemed like a good idea.

Do You Need A Quality Video?

We can help, your project reliably delivered by a highly skilled, friendly team of experts

wowvideo production

Contents

What You Need To Know & What You Don't

All currently available books on video production teach you how to produce videos. That's great if you're a creative or technical person either already in, or aspiring to be in, the industry.

However, as a company executive looking to have a video produced for you, you simply don't need to know the technical side of how to operate a camera, record sound correctly or how to use editing software.

But you do need to be familiar with the production processes, and matters which concern you at an executive level.

This book will teach you only that which you need to know, and it will empower you to manage a production effectively whist making educated project decisions to ultimately ensure your project is delivered exactly how you require it.

Choosing The Right Production Company For Your Needs

When commissioning a video production, the most critical task you will face is choosing the right company to produce it for you.

Making the right decision is crucial because the success of the project will ultimately depend on that company's skill and ability to deliver exactly what you require.

At face value, video production companies each offer the same product.

However, this is not necessarily the case. Depending on the video, there will be a variety of factors which determine whether or not it will be an overall success.

Examples of which include:

- The video's ability to influence the audience to follow a desired line of thought
- The video's ability to persuade the target audience to take a desired course of action
- How favourably your product, service or business is ultimately perceived by the target audience after having watched the video

- The video's ability to successfully communicate key principles or information
- To communicate:
- Succinctly
- In a style that the target audience will best respond to
- By avoiding the use of unexplained technical jargon
- By explaining new ideas, concepts and technical features in such a way that the target audience will be able to appreciate and comprehend

That list is by no means exhaustive. But as you can see, the successful production of a video relies on a lot more than just a series of nicely filmed pictures.

A brief video show reel of previous productions is commonly the main sales and marketing tool which video production companies use to attract new business. And for most executives, seeing a series of good quality video clips in quick succession is an effective convincer.

However, for the more discerning buyer, this is where the task of selecting the right production company becomes a challenge. This is because the work which is actually responsible for making a successful video is largely carried out in the pre-production process. Video show reels are typically designed to dazzle and impress, rather than to demonstrate quality of content, which is why they cannot be used as a reliable indicator as to whether or not your video will perform as you need it.

Your video project will and should be unique, which is why the Producer you select will have to carry out a detailed consultation.

Note: With a wealth of options available, you should discount anyone who doesn't make the effort to consult with you properly on the full scope of your project, and in turn deliver a detailed, custom made project proposal.

They should be discounted simply because it can be taken as indicative of their approach of dealing with you as a client and the way they will handle your project.

You are not only looking to appoint an expert in the field of video production, but someone who will share the same level of commitment in wanting to do everything possible to make sure your video is a success, as determined by any number of the previously listed points.

During a consultation you need to be sure that *your* needs are listened to first and foremost. Following on from that, that you are offered considered advice *after* finding out what your needs, goals and objectives are.

Another thing which you will need to be confident about is that the production company in question has the personnel, skill and ability to deliver your project to the standard you need and within the time frame you specify. To verify this you should ask:

- Who will be working on your project?
- How are they qualified to work on the project?
- What previous examples of similar work have they produced?
- How will they manage the delivery of the project?

Ultimately the proposal should be a confirmation of everything you have discussed during your consultation as well as further elaboration on key points where appropriate.

If you are in any doubt whatsoever, or you would like further input, you must request clarification. A good Producer will not mind this in the slightest. This is because you need to be 100% confident and happy in your decision.

The Production Process Overview

The production of a video is carried out over a number of stages: Pre-production, Production and Post-production. Each of these stages are broken down into individual tasks.

It is common for these individual tasks to need to be performed sequentially, requiring the previous one to be completed in full before progressing. During the pre-production meeting with your Producer, he or she will establish your project's production plan and highlight any tasks which will require a previous one to be completed before the project can advance.

Here is an overview for a typical project and the various processes one will likely involve:

Pre-production

- Budgeting
- Initial Consultation
- Pre-production Meeting
- Briefing of Stakeholders & Contributors
- Concept Development
- Content Development
- Script Development
- Location Search & Arrangement

- Location Visits
- Media Collation
- Storyboarding
- Talent Search & Selection
- Contributor Booking
- Film shoot Booking

Production

- Animation & Graphics
- Voice Over Recording
- Filming

Post-production

- Editing
- Music Licensing & Sound Design
- Picture & Colour Grading
- Sound Mixing
- Subtitling & British Sign Language (BSL)
- Foreign Language Versioning
- Reviewing, Feedback & Amendments
- Final Delivery

Pre-production

Budgeting

Before engaging with a production company you will need to have at the very least, a budget range in mind or better yet, a pre-allocated budget.

This is necessary because every video production is unique in one way or another, and costings will in turn vary. If a Producer knows how much or how little he has to work with, he will then be able to come back with a series of suggestions or a solid plan for how your video can be produced within your budget.

If you don't have any idea as to how much you might need to allocate or request as a budget, there is a very useful pricing guide which you can download for free from here:

http://wowvideoproduction.co.uk/pricing/

The guide gives you example productions which can be produced for different budget ranges.

As with any project of this nature, no matter how well planned or executed, during the course of production unexpected expenses may well arise, as might the need to adapt the original plan for the overall benefit of the project. This is why you should include provision for a contingency budget.

Typically around 10% of the overall project cost is a well advised figure, but for productions under £8,000 a contingency budget of 20% is recommended.

A contingency budget will help cover you against additional production items which may crop up such as:

- Additional cast or extras
- Additional site visits
- Crew overtime if a shooting day runs over its allotted time
- Last-minute cancellation fees
- Production of extra graphics and animation

Initial Consultation

The initial consultation is carried out before the project is formally commissioned.

The consultation is necessary to establish the scope of the project and to produce a detailed project proposal.

During initial consultation meetings and telephone calls, a detailed scope of the project will be established. This will include key information relating to your business, your marketplace, why you want a video, and ultimately what you need that video to either do or what you need it for.

It is common for much more detailed project information to be established.

Information such as:

- The approach or style of the video to be produced
- Techniques to be used
- Content and locations for filming

All of this information will provide an excellent foundation and briefing for the following pre-production meeting.

Pre-production Meeting

The pre-production meeting is the single most important meeting of the project. All project stakeholders and topic experts should be present.

A topic expert is typically someone within your company or organisation whose knowledge will be integral to the development of the content and or script.

The meeting should be chaired by your Producer and will follow a defined structure relative to your project that will be sure to garner all necessary information, establish tasks and points for discussion, as well as exploring ideas, methods and styles for production.

A well-managed production meeting is incredibly rewarding for all those involved. As the commissioning executive it's particularly rewarding because you will be directly involved in the development of the concept. Following the meeting you will have a very clear idea and vision as to how the project will take shape and how it will ultimately look.

Furthermore, both you and your team will have a clearly defined series of tasks to be followed up directly after the meeting.

Briefing of Stakeholders & Contributors

The pre-production meeting will have identified contributors whose input will be necessary for the project. Additionally, there may well be stakeholders who were either not able to attend the preproduction meeting, or who were identified as persons who should be stakeholders in the project.

These persons will each need introducing to the project as well as requesting their involvement in advance of them providing input.

Concept Development

The concept of the video covers a wide range of features including, but not limited to:

- The style of video
- The content to be communicated
- Whether animation will be used, and if so, what style of animation and what its content will be
- Liaison with contributors
- Identification of filming opportunities and locations
- Selecting specialist filming techniques or equipment, such as super slow motion cameras and aerial photography
- Determining any required alternative adaptations, such as foreign language versions, subtitling, or alternative edits for different audiences
- Identification of graphics, imagery, video and audio clips which would be of benefit if they were included

Content Development

Once commissioned, the Producer will work directly with yourself as commissioning executive. If the project requires it, he will also work with the appropriate content specialist at your company to assist in the content development. In large companies this may well involve a team of people across various areas of the business.

The content specialist will know the material, but may not know the best way to clearly present it, both visually and audibly, to the target audience.

Devising how to communicate content clearly, and effectively, is the core skill of a good Producer and it is their job to make sure this happens.

One of the golden rules in producing effective videos for business is to make sure your content is focused on the viewer at all times.

This means you should communicate in terms of benefits to the viewer, or to focus on their interests, needs, wants, aspirations or desires.

Above all else as the production expression goes, "Content is King." The content of what you say or show is the real reason why you set about having a video produced in the first place. As such, all other aspects of production are subsidiary when compared to the development of the video's content.

The content development process typically comes before the development of the script. Script development is covered in the next section.

Because creative projects are fluid by nature, the concept may continue to be developed as the script takes form.

The next step in the content and development process is to determine how it will be communicated. Options for this include:

- Filmed Footage (location or studio)
- Animation
- Graphics
- Presenter Piece To Camera
- Voice-over
- Interview
- Testimonials
- Acting
- Panel Discussion
- Vox Pops (questions to the general public)
- Stock Footage

Script Development

With all of the information gathered from the pre-production work to date, your Producer will then be able to develop the first draft of the script. In certain cases a separate script writer will be brought on board who will work directly with the Producer in producing the script.

As the dedicated Producer he will have an intimate knowledge of all the information and specifications relating to the project, and as a result will be able to produce a first draft which will require minimal further development.

Following the first draft, both you and your team will be able to provide feedback. Your Producer will take this on board in script review meetings to further develop the script based on the feedback provided.

The script development process can be prone to being a drawn-out affair if multiple stakeholders are involved.

A key way of mitigating against this is through the initial briefing given to stakeholders and contributors where they are made aware of the importance of giving feedback on the script input as soon as they can, once a draft is available.

Commonly, deadlines are given to contributors for when feedback must be submitted. This approach is preferable as it helps keep a project on schedule.

Location Search & Arrangement

With some projects, establishing where filming will take place will be relatively straightforward, whilst for others the process may involve a reasonable amount of deliberation.

If a location is not known to you or the film crew, a location visit may well be advisable and necessary. Location visits are covered in the next section.

Your Producer should highlight a series of considerations when putting forward potential filming locations. Such considerations include whether or not other locations will be able to be filmed at on the same day, or whether constraints such as travel and set up time mean that a particular location needs a day or more dedicating to it.

In these eventualities your Producer will provide you with alternatives so that you can make a considered decision with the knowledge of the full facts clearly presented to you.

Once you've decided on the location(s), appropriate permissions and clearance for filming will then need to be arranged.

Filming on privately owned property will of course need the owner's or managing agent's permission. Certain 'public' areas will also need special permission, and often incur a fee for doing so.

Such examples include the Royal Parks (Hyde Park, Regent's Park etc), Piccadilly Circus and Leicester Square. Canary Wharf in London is also a location which is commonly thought of as being public, although in fact the site is entirely privately owned and managed by Canary Wharf plc. Filming here together with permissions to do so are entirely at their discretion.

Your Producer should allow a few weeks lead time in which to make appropriate arrangements and in certain cases pay a nominal location filming fee.

Your Producer will take care of all of this for you and include the provision of risk assessments, method statements and public liability insurance, all of which fall under the responsibility of the production company.

Location Visits

When location filming is involved, a location visit prior to the filming date(s) may be necessary.

A location visit is generally required if there are questions about the suitability of the location for the shoot. Similarly, if there are specific and complicated shots needed, or a wide variety of shots and scenes to be filmed. An exploratory location visit will facilitate the smooth running of filming on the day by ensuring that all required content can be filmed.

Understandably, if the location visit reveals problems with the proposed shoot or the location does not provide the shots required, then there will be time to make alternative arrangements.

Prior to booking filming dates, all persons need to be confident that location filming will go to plan and the crew will be able to film exactly what is required. One of the golden rules of successful video producing is that if there is ever any doubt over arrangements for a filming location, then a location visit should be undertaken.

The project's costings and budget are at the forefront of any commissioning executive's mind. The cost of a single person location visit is always significantly cheaper than that of the entire film crew and cast being required to film on an additional replacement day.

Some caution can be economically worthwhile.

A well costed production proposal will include a contingency budget. Therefore, if an additional location visit is later identified as being required, it should not prove to be a problem.

Media Collation

Media collation involves the gathering of all logos, graphics and artwork which will be required during the editing process.

Media items commonly come from a number of contacts including external agencies and suppliers. Depending on quantity and complexity of the requirements, this can easily take a few weeks to arrange.

This is why a well-managed video project attends to these matters as early as possible and all media is successfully assembled well in advance of editing. With all media to hand, the editor will be able to begin editing exactly on schedule.

Storyboarding

Storyboarding is the process of pictorially illustrating the video shot by shot, with captioning for every shot.

A storyboard does an excellent job of demonstrating how the video is set to look like before it is produced or filmed. A storyboard is essential if the video contains, or is wholly comprised, of animation.

With the proposed content laid out, it can then be discussed with all stakeholders on the project. It may also highlight any discrepancies or areas for improvement. In which case, they can easily be worked on and the agreed changes put into place for review, with the ultimate storyboard sign off once everyone is happy with what they see before them.

Storyboards are not always required, although this will entirely depending on the scope of your project.

Talent Search & Selection

If actors, presenters, extras and a voice-over artist are required for your project, a process of search and selection will be required.

The first step will be in identifying what the project needs and what you want. For example, the project may need a presenter to host the video as well as a separate voice-over artist to narrate other sections of the video.

With on screen talent (actors, presenters and extras) to help with the selection process you will collectively identify gender, age and any other physical or personal characteristics you would prefer.

The same process will apply to the specification of requirements for a voice-over artist with you deciding which age, gender and accent you would like.

Your Producer will then be able to research and come back with a series of suggestions for talent which matches your requirements.

When considering actors and presenters you will be presented with either their publicity photos, their video show reel or both.

For a more in-depth assessment of their suitability you can request them to record a brief demo video of them acting out a section of the script or delivering a piece to camera if they are presenting. This is commonly done without charge, although not always.

Depending on the production you may be advised by your Producer to carry out a test shoot. This can be particularly useful if you are experimenting with a concept or would like to see how actors interact with each other on screen. A test shoot is done with a minimal film crew and depending on the size of the project the talent may or may not make a charge for attending.

Voice-over artists will each have an audio demo reel which you will be able to audition. Your Producer will also be able to arrange for shortlisted voice-over artists to record a section of the script for you to assess more accurately how the finished piece will sound like. As before, there may or may not be a small charge made by the artists for this.

It is recommended that during the talent selection process you have at least one or two options in case your favourite is not available when you require it.

Performers are typically self-employed, which means that they will accept confirmed bookings on a first-come first-served basis. One of the problems which can arise is that if filming dates are not confirmed at the time of selecting talent, someone else may book them for that date in the meantime.

Contributor Booking

Contributors are people who are to be interviewed or featured in the video. They can also be specialist or technical advisers. The input of advisers is concerned with making sure that the recorded content is accurate or in line with company policy.

Pre-production work will include liaising with contributors so that they will be able to attend on the days required. The Producer or Production Assistant will ensure that each contributor is fully briefed on what input they are to provide, as well as timings, location details, and if applicable travel and accommodation arrangements.

Sometimes filming dates and entire schedules may have to be revisited if a key contributor's schedule does not fit in with the proposed production schedule. This is why it is preferable to identify and liaise with contributors as early as possible.

Film Shoot Booking

A video shoot commonly has to be arranged around either a date whenever filming has to happen, or when there is good weather.

Filming on a specific date may be required if that is the only time a key contributor is available, or an event is scheduled to take place which you need to film.

Depending on the time of year, you may be fortunate to enjoy an extended spell of good weather through the dates you need to film on. However, in the name of effective production planning you will need to make a decision as to which holds the most importance

- either filming on a specific date, or having good weather to film in.

Bad weather generally only affects filming which takes place outdoors. One of the ways in which complications caused by bad weather can be mitigated against includes having alternative filming plans where filming can take place indoors if the weather is bad.

Five day weather forecasts are the only ones which can be relied upon. Forecasts longer than that can be useful, although they are far from an exact science.

An important point to bear in mind is that if a pre-booked film shoot has to be cancelled with seven days' notice or less, cancellation fees will be applicable in the majority of cases.

With good production planning the chances of a shoot needing to be cancelled and rescheduled can be minimised. In the case of medium to large size productions, separate insurance policies are available to help mitigate against any significant losses.

Filming in the UK during winter not only has increased risk of bad weather, but the amount of daylight filming hours and quality of daylight is also greatly reduced. It is for this reason that foreign location filming becomes a viable and attractive option if budgets allow.

South Africa is a particularly good choice of location because of its stable sunny weather offering extended daylight filming hours.

Your Producer will take care of all arrangements for booking the film shoot. Where appropriate, he or she will consult with you for advice or help with authorisation.

Production

Animation & Graphics

Animation has an incredibly wide scope for what it can be used for, being available in two different varieties; 2D and 3D.

2D animation is flat in appearance and is commonly used where the technical explanation of a principle or concept is the focus.

In 3D animation, anything is possible. Whilst it costs more to produce than 2D because of the increased amount of man hours needed, the results can be thoroughly impressive.

With 3D animation, you can produce photorealistic objects and scenes with exceptional quality and detail.

The production of animation is very labour intensive, and charged for by the hour. It is for this reason that a careful approach to producing animation needs to be taken.

The following graphic details the animation production workflow. Each individual process requires sign off by you, the client, before proceeding to the next production process.

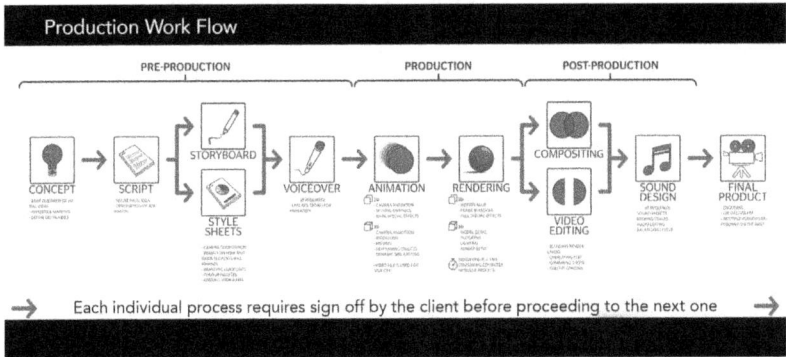

Production Work Flow

PRE-PRODUCTION • PRODUCTION • POST-PRODUCTION

Each individual process requires sign off by the client before proceeding to the next one

If the animation production workflow is not respected and followed carefully, then production costs can easily spiral out of control. The reason for this is because the animation process is incredibly labour-intensive. Rendering is where the computer processes all of the information provided by the animation programme to ultimately produce the animated video. Because of the detail and complexity of an animation, to produce it in a reasonable amount of time the rendering process may require a series of computers, also known as a render farm.

You will be able to preview low resolution copies of the animation without any additional cost.

Because render time on large projects can be quite costly, this is why it is essential to be sure the animation is exactly as you want it before it is rendered in full.

Voice Over Recording

A voice over is sometimes referred to as a narration, and this is provided by a voice-over artist. Once your script has been signed off it can then be sent off to be recorded. This can be done in one of several ways.

1: The voice-over artist records the script in their own time at their studio, and follows guidance relating to style and the speed in which it needs to be read.

2: The voice-over artist records the script remotely from their studio with the Producer, and yourself (optional), listening in over the telephone to ensure the correct style is provided. In between takes progress can be discussed and adapted as necessary.

3: The production team attend the studio recording with the voice-over artist in person.

The first option is typically the quickest and most cost-effective. However, your Producer will be happy to discuss and advise on which method would be most suitable for your project.

Filming

Whilst the process of filming speaks for itself, this is a good time to quickly cover the key pieces of filming equipment that can make a significant difference to a production.

Grip equipment is anything which helps move or stabilise the camera.

Whenever grip equipment is used, a video will look more polished and engaging.

Steadicam and Movi are trade names of specialised equipment which facilitate the stabilisation of a camera whilst moving along uneven terrain. Specialist operators are required to do this so as to make a camera seemingly glide through the air.

Particularly for shots which last a long time, this equipment is fantastic for adding dynamism to them.

Cranes and jibs allow a camera to be elevated and moved through the air in a controlled fashion. You would most likely associate this with grand movie style 'money shots.' Whilst shots from a crane and a jib should be used sparingly in a video, they greatly increase its production values.

Aerial filming drones, depending on the skill of the operators, are able to provide complex and thoroughly impressive moving aerial shots. Previously, these types of shots would only have been possible for high end television and movie productions which could afford a helicopter charter. Filming with aerial drones can often be a preferred choice to cranes because of the increased variety of shots they can offer.

An important point to make here is that professionally piloted and equipped filming drones are a league apart from the commonly available prosumer drones which wedding videographers often use.

Post Production

Editing

Editing is the process of assembling all of the media content to produce the video as set out on the storyboard and is another particularly labour intensive endeavour.

As soon as it is ready, you will be able to view your video online. You and your team will be able to give feedback and make requests for amendments from which a revised draft provided will then be produced. This process will be repeated until you are completely happy with the finished product.

Music Licensing & Sound Design

The inclusion of music and featuring of sound effects in a production can be done in one of two ways.

Pre-produced audio content can be used or adapted and subsequently licensed for your project. Alternatively, music can be especially written and sound effects custom recorded. Understandably, custom created content comes at a premium.

The path you choose will be strongly influenced by your budget. There is no right or wrong answer as to which option to select as there is a seemingly endless catalogue of pre-produced music and sound effects which can be used and adapted for your production.

If budget is not an issue a common deciding factor would be whether or not you feel the pre-produced examples are a good fit for your video.

Regular audio content will be licensed subject to restrictions. As part of the licensing process you will need to specify where your video will be shown and over which period. For example, the video may be included on your website indefinitely, or projected on to a screen as part of a month long series of seminar talks. Pricing will then be determined based on that information.

The alternative is what is known as 'buy out / royalty free' audio. That means only a single one-off fee will be charged and you are then free to have your video played wherever you desire and for as long as you want.

Picture & Colour Grading

Picture grading involves fine tuning each shot in your video to ensure consistency. Once pictures have been graded, they can then be colour graded. This process is more of an artistic one, individual scenes can be given individual looks, or the whole video can be given its own unique colour stylised look.

Sound Mixing

Sound mixing is the process of ensuring individual sound sources are at the desired level and that there are no blemishes to the sound.

Subtitling and British Sign Language (BSL)

Subtitling your video can serve a wide variety of uses and provide a range of benefits. It may be required if:

- A person speaking is in a noisy environment, or has a heavy regional or foreign accent
- If the audio will not be clearly heard when the video is played back. For example, at an exhibition or waiting room
- You want to cater for persons who are either hard of hearing or deaf

There are two types of subtitling. The first is regular subtitling where words are displayed on screen at the same time as they are spoken.

The other is known as 'closed captioning.' Closed captions describe all significant audio content and spoken dialogue, including who is speaking and if appropriate, in what manner.

The Disability Discrimination Act in the UK requires that all content and information produced by a company be accessible to all.

Medium to large sized companies are much more likely to come under scrutiny for this, although smaller companies should still regard this as being of concern.

Both subtitling and close captioning are actually relatively inexpensive. In addition to complying with the Disability Discrimination Act by having your video subtitled or closed captioned, it will then be accessible to an even larger audience.

BSL is the preferred language of deaf people in the UK. Videos are subtitled with BSL by overlaying a sign language interpreter on top of the original video.

Foreign Language Versioning

You may need to have your video understood by foreign-language speakers. There are two different ways in which this can be approached:

- The first, and most common, is to have foreign language subtitling
- The second is to have a foreign language voice over

Foreign language subtitling is the more common of the two, and is less expensive than the other option.

Accuracy in this field is key because of the many embarrassing and potentially damaging implications of words or thoughts which an inaccurate translation may pose.

As an additional potential complication many European and Asian languages, when translated directly from English, are 15% to 20% more expansive. This means that a 3'00 minute video would have a foreign script which runs to 3'36 in duration.

To accommodate this a video script translator will ideally need to be a native language speaker so as to be able to keep the original context, communicate the same key points, and do so in line with the restricted timing.

Reviewing, Feedback & Amendments

When you receive the first draft of the finished piece, this will be for you to review the content and story.

This is your opportunity to check that the content has been conveyed in the right manner, that there are no technical inaccuracies and to ensure that the video as a whole works.

At this point the sound will not have been mixed fully and certain shots may be lighter or darker than others. This is because the edit needs to be signed off before it has the sound and pictures perfected. The perfecting of audio is simply known as a sound mix, while the pictures go through a process called 'grading' as previously covered.

If multiple stakeholders are involved your Producer will wait until all feedback has been received before taking it on board and making any necessary changes.

Sometimes there can be conflicts in the feedback received and your Producer will assist you in deriving a definitive answer for the direction to be followed.

After all amendments have been agreed and completed, final project sign-off is requested and the master video file can then be supplied.

It's important to recognise however, that once final sign-off has been given, no further changes will be possible within the scope of the project. That is to say that any future revisions or amendments would be chargeable as extra work.

Storage, Future Adaptations & Updates

After project sign-off, the project is complete. However, at a later date you may wish to have the video updated for a variety of reasons.

You should ensure that you receive the full resolution master file of the finished product. The master file of a short video will typically be several gigabytes in size.

If the video you receive is only a few megabytes or a few hundred megabytes, the chances are that it is a compressed version which will be fine for internet delivery, but it will not be the full master file.

In case you wish to revise your video(s) at a future date, the best practice is to have a live version of your project kept on file. This will involve storage of all the project media which will commonly be several hundreds of gigabytes in size on a dedicated hard drive.

Your video production company should be able to provide you with a storage service so that future edits can be done easily and cost effectively.

Final Delivery

The final delivery of your video files will typically be done online through a large file transfer service. Alternatively your video production company may provide it to you on a physical storage device.

Prior to the outputting of your final file(s) you should be able to ask for your video to be encoded in any special format that you may need. For example, if you have a company intranet your IT team may need a certain file type such as a WMV at a specific picture size and bit rate. Similarly, if you intend presenting it on an iPad or laptop during presentations you may need to have a reduced file size version of the video. Your video production company will be able to provide all of this for you.

Production Staff

Here is a breakdown of members of the production team who are used in producing business videos.

Producer

Whilst you are the client, the Producer is the commander-in-chief of the production. It is their job to fully familiarise themselves with your business, marketplace, goals and objectives.

He or she should be your primary point of contact throughout the production because of their understanding of the project and connections to all involved, including production staff.

The Producer will develop both the concept and content with you. They will often script the video for you, whilst in other circumstances a specialist script writer will be required.

All other suggestions, arrangements and work needing to be done will be carried out or delegated by the Producer.

Script Writer

The script writer's sole purpose is to produce the video's script. They will work closely with both the Producer and yourself to research all necessary content. Depending on the production they may need to speak directly with the appropriate content specialists at your company. They may also need to carry out further research in whichever direction it takes to be able to produce the scripts your project needs.

Director

On small to mid-sized video productions, the Director and the Producer are often the same person. On larger productions the Director will be a separate person for reasons given below.

The Director's role is to lead creative staff to bring the concept to life, and in-turn, the script.

A Director will start work on the project after the concept has been established. His work can include the direction of the production of graphics, animation and sound as well as the selection of talent such as actors and voice-over artists.

On the day of filming the Director will be in charge of proceedings including talent and crew members.

Director of Photography / Cameraman

A Director of Photography (DOP) and a cameraman are two separate roles, although fundamentally they perform the same role.

What sets them apart is their level of expertise and creative input into the project.

A DOP is responsible for creatively suggesting shots in line with the requirements of the Director or storyboard. He will also choose which lenses to use in order to achieve the desired look as well operating the camera itself. The DOP's right hand man is the Lighting Technician who illuminates scenes according to the DOP's requirements.

A cameraman will still be able to frame shots and operate the camera. However, their overall creativity and ability to direct the lighting of a scene will not be as skilled as a DOP.

Lighting Technician (gaffer)

The lighting requirements for a shoot can vary from a basic setup such as a single person interview up to an entire studio or large location.

The Lighting Technician is often referred to as the 'gaffer.' He will help specify the lighting requirements prior to the shoot as well as how it should be powered as regular mains electricity supplies are only suitable for basic setups.

On the day of the shoot the Lighting Technician, possibly helped by assistants, will be responsible for the transportation, set up and operation of all lighting.

Sound Recordist

People rarely comment on good sound, but they do notice poor quality audio.

This is why the Sound Recordist is one of the unsung heroes of a production.

He will get involved just prior to the shoot to ensure he has the correct equipment the conditions of filming requires in order to do the job well.

The Sound Recordist will take care of fitting any wearable microphones that presenters and actors may need. On small to mid-size productions they will also operate an overhead sound boom if required. On large productions a Boom Operator (Sound Assistant) will be dedicated to that role.

During recording he will closely monitor the sound to ensure the correct volume is recorded as well as highlighting any problems, such as unwanted noises, which would require the scene to be reshot for the benefit of good audio.

Assistants (camera, lighting, sound)

Assistants in these three creative areas provide excellent value for money on a production.

The most time consuming aspect of a shoot is the setting up of equipment for a shot, moving on to the next one, and the packing away of equipment afterwards.

This is why assistants helping to get this done as quickly as possible are so valuable as more filming will be able to be produced in a day. When taking into account the total cost of a day's shoot, the cost of the assistants' fees are negligible given that they can quite easily be responsible for facilitating two days' worth of filming in just the one.

Production Assistant

A Production Assistant will not have a specific technical role to fulfil, instead he or she will provide general assistance before and during the production, reporting to either the Producer or Director.

Hair & Make-up Technicians

Hair and Make-up Technicians are often the difference between a somewhat amateur looking video production and a professional one.

On camera, under lighting a person's appearance comes under much greater scrutiny which is why this role deserves serious consideration.

Both men and women can benefit from make up. Whilst women frequently receive more attention, both can benefit from blemishes being either minimised or hidden.

Shine on a person's face caused by perspiration or excess oil production is just as much a problem for men as women.

A Make-up Technician will have a variety of products to manage this and it is something that they will monitor closely, often taking the opportunity between takes to reapply as necessary.

A Hair Technician's role is to expertly style the hair of presenters, actors and extras on the day.

For productions where heavy styling or large numbers of people need attending to, there will be a separate Hair Technician, possibly supported by assistants.

Over the past few years there has been a major development in the field of make-up, called HD make up. This is applied by an airbrush, quite literally photo-shopping in real life and is invisible to the naked eye.

HD make up is of particular benefit when filming in 4K Ultra HD because of the incredible level of detail of 4K Ultra HD video.

Presenter / Actor / Extras

Presenters are used to introduce and host a video. It is worth noting that presenting and acting are two separate skill sets.

Actors and extras are used to bring visual scenes to life, making them more interesting or they can be used to act out entire dialogue driven scenes.

Choosing the right talent for your video can be of paramount importance. This process is covered in a later section of this book.

Project Management

Excellent project management is absolutely essential to the successful delivery of your video project.

If you identify a Producer as having good project management skills and you later choose to work with them, your life as a client will be made ever so much easier.

This will be because you will not be faced with unexpected and rushed deadlines, the risk of mistake will be minimised, and you will maintain a good working relationship with your colleagues by not having to burden them with last minute urgent requests.

Particularly where multiple stakeholders are involved in the development & sign off of projects, it is imperative that crossed communications and delays are avoided.

In the interests of managing a video project as effectively and efficiently as possible, it is highly desirable to use an online project management system. There are numerous benefits to this approach, some of which include:

- A centralised list of project stages and tasks
- Individuals know exactly which tasks they are responsible for delivering
- Start and due dates for each task are clearly known by all

- Information is easily accessible by all parties from mobiles, tablets or desktop computers
- All data is securely protected against computer failure through being cloud-based
- Project members are instantly updated when tasks are completed or further input is required

A caveat of a good online project management system is that is has to be simple and intuitive to use. This is because both you and your colleagues will not be able to spend any great length of time learning another computerised system for use over a relatively short period.

The following are some screenshots of the video project management system we use at WOW Video Production. They readily meet the criteria of being both intuitive and easy to learn.

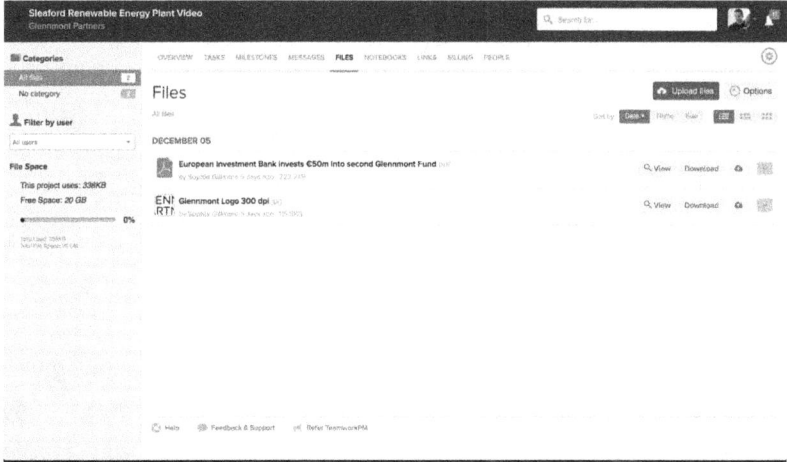

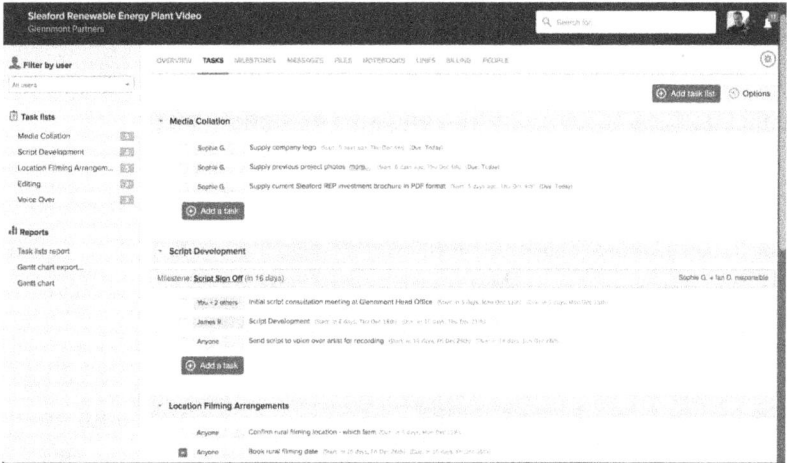

Overall, the reason why you should make sure your project is managed through an online system is because room for error, or failure to hit key deadlines, is thoroughly minimised as it is clear who has to do what and by when. It also provides an audit trail of all communications and work.

Quality of Equipment

The quality of equipment which a production company uses has a huge bearing on the quality of the finished product.

A variety of factors will determine which equipment any given production company has. The first will be down to how much they chose to invest in equipment in the first place. The biggest single investment will be the camera itself, which can cost anywhere between £2,000 for a 'prosumer' camera (the midpoint between a consumer and professional piece of equipment), up to around £90,000 for a true top of the range professional camera.

Those figures exclude the cost of lenses and other equipment such as battery packs, storage media and tripods, all of which can quite easily cost as much as the camera itself depending where on the scale you are.

The other factor is how old the equipment is and what equipment upgrade policy a company has. With standards and video quality constantly being improved and entirely new formats released periodically, a healthy approach for renewing equipment is around the five-year mark.

However, it's not uncommon for companies to keep hold of their equipment for up to ten years. The problem with this is that work produced using this equipment will look inferior to what is currently able to be produced, and videos produced on old equipment will look dated to the point of needing to be re-filmed not too long after the video is produced.

Regular High Definition at the time of writing this book, April 2015, is currently being superseded by 4K Ultra HD. Both terms relate to the quality of a video picture and 4K offers video resolution four times greater than regular HD. As a result, the improvement in picture quality is significant.

Previously the upgrade cycle in video was driven by when consumers upgraded their television sets. However, laptops tablets and mobile phones are leading the upgrade process because the ownership life cycle of these devices is much shorter than compared with a home TV set. This year in particular, we will see many more of those devices supporting 4K Ultra HD video playback and users will expect to be served 4K Ultra HD video content.

Unless your video is intended to have a particularly short lifespan, you should avoid producing anything in regular HD from now on because it will soon look dated.

When filming in 4K it is important it is also edited in 4K Ultra HD. During this transitional period, even if the finished video is delivered in regular HD, the reason why filming in 4K is so important relates to the quality and size of the image sensor in the camera.

With larger image sensors, 4K cameras record much bigger pictures with much clearer resolution. This is similar to how your current stills camera produces notably better pictures than the one you had ten years ago.

Project Planning

The planning of project timescales is most effectively done when using a Gantt chart.

A Gantt chart is a visual planning medium which allows project leaders to effortlessly plan individual task start and finish times as well as entire stages for the benefit of the accurate and timely delivery of the overall project.

Here is an example of what a Gantt chart looks like:

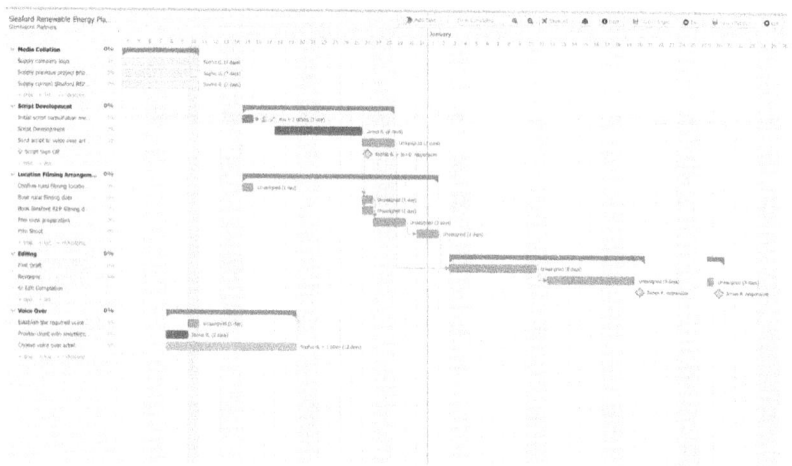

Individual tasks will often need to be completed before a following one may be started. In project planning terms this is known as a dependency.

On a Gantt chart a dependency is illustrated as an arrow pointing from one task item to the next. If an online Gantt chart is used, such as within an online project management system. If an individual task start or completion date needs to be moved, then the chart will automatically update. It will instantly show you the knock-on effect which that change has, and if the ultimate delivery date has been affected.

It's important to always allow sufficient time for an individual task to be completed. Sometimes a task may be a simple one, but if it requires the input of someone else in your company who has a particularly busy schedule, then this should be accounted for and a realistic amount of time attributed.

On the subject of the input and help from other staff members being required. As mentioned earlier in this book, this is why briefing contributors at the beginning of a project as to how their later help and input will be needed at a later date is good practice. This is because when that time arrives they will already be partly prepared..

Planning Filming Days

Care should be taken when scheduling and planning film days. Your Producer will take the lead on this and consult with you in the process.

A key mistake to avoid is to not try and cram too much filming into any single day.

Sufficient time with a run-over buffer should be planned for each scene or shot. The same should apply to ensuring there is enough time to safely move from one location to another.

Changes in location typically cause the most delay and further risk of complications.

Other non-filming elements can eat into time but still need to be accounted for, such as:

- Industrial plants or construction sites where detailed Health and Safety briefings need to be provided for all visiting contractors.
- Where parking is not immediately close to the filming location, or where the crew can safely and securely store equipment so as to set up a temporary operating base.
- The need for any staff members to meet or chaperone the film crew. It is imperative that they are not only punctual, but arrive in advance. This is to avoid any unexpected

delays on their part such as traffic problems. Their late arrival, no matter how understandable or genuine, will in the worst scenario be responsible for the film crew not having enough time to film what is required. As a result, an extra day's worth of filming may be needed, which will be directly accountable to you, the client.

Production Economies

Here is a selection of some of the key ways in which you can save money in a video production.

Parking: Any parking charges are passed a long at cost which is why this is a quick and easy money saver if you can arrange for parking to be provided.

Order of filming: Because changes in location tend to take a considerable amount of time, good production planning dictates that the number of location changes should be minimised. Video is typically not shot in sequence, so moving sections to be filmed around between days or different times of the day makes no difference at all.

Overtime: A standard filming day is ten hours, which includes breaks and lunch time. A ten hour day filming is a long day's work and is invariably tiring.

On occasion, filming time will, for whatever reason, run over the standard ten hours. At that point overtime becomes applicable and that is to be charged at time and a half.

Overtime should be monitored and handled very carefully not just for the extra cost implications, but because of the fatigue experienced by the crew. In situations that require it, a good film crew will always pull together to get the job done. But you will always get much better results from a crew which is both well looked after and well rested.

Assistants: Production Assistants in technical and general supportive roles provide excellent value for money and are directly responsible for facilitating more filming to be done in a day. So whilst their salary will be an expenditure, specifying to have the right amount of Production Assistants can ultimately save significant amounts of money when taking into account the overall cost of a full day's film shoot.

Getting work right first time: Scripts and storyboards are signed off by you and your team once you are happy with their content.

This means that no further changes will be possible following that point without additional charge. It's rare that anything is not able to be changed if it is later realised as being necessary.

A good example of this is when the script gets sent off to be voiced over. Before a script is sent to the voice-over artist, a client will physically sign off that they are happy with the script and no further changes are necessary.

The voice-over artist then records the script and sends it back. What happens fairly often is that is a factual error is noticed by someone previously not involved with the project and the scripts needs to be adjusted accordingly. The script can easily be changed, however the voice-over artist will then bill that as a separate job because he or she will have delivered exactly what was previously required.

As mentioned, it's hardly the end of the world as these things can be put right. However, in the interests of avoiding any unnecessary extra costs and ultimately saving money, this is why focused attention should be given to making sure that everything is in order and correct when scripts and storyboards are signed off.

Legal & Licensing

A permission to film is the first item to be considered if filming on location on private land. Checks should also be made on other areas which at first are thought to be public, but still require official permission such as the Royal Parks, Leicester Square and Piccadilly Circus.

Your Producer will take care of all of this for you, although it is something that you should at least be aware of, and that time and in some cases additional fees will be required to facilitate that filming.

Participant releases are required for anyone who appears and is clearly identifiable in your video. This can include both members of the public as well as your own staff.

A participant release gives written authority that you are free to use the person's image and sound in your production, and that no payment will be applicable unless agreed.

It is important that these releases are properly managed and signed because without them a person can demand that they are later removed from your video and possibly seek compensation as a result. A participant release form will also protect you against employees who are featured in the video, and later request to be removed from the video. A signed release form however will at the very least leave that to your discretion if you would like to comply.

Presenters, actors and voice-over artists often require negotiations regarding licensing for usage. Typically this will involve how long will the video will be used for.

Usage periods are broken down into periods of either 1,2,3,5 years, or in perpetuity. The longer the usage, the greater the fee.

If your video is ever likely to be used on television separate negotiations from remuneration will either need to be made upfront or at a later date.

A common and often preferable alternative to licensing is to agree what is known as a 'buy out fee.' This means that there will be a one-off fee for their performance for an agreed medium of usage, for example online and mobile usage only.

Insurance, Health & Safety

Health and safety compliance together with insurance are two key areas which you need to ensure your appointed video production company has effective policies in place for, and manages them effectively. In addition, they need to have adequate, current insurance protection.

For your own protection as well as your company's brand and organisation, you should make a point of going through the production company's approach to health and safety risk management. That should include making sure you receive copies of their method statements and risk assessments prior to a filming engagement.

Checking to see that they have adequate, current insurance documentation is also important. The industry standard, and therefore minimum amount of cover which you should accept, is a £2 million public liability insurance policy.

Diligence on your part to carry out these checks can be very quick and easy. But the peace of mind that both the public and your company is adequately protected is invaluable. It also provides you with protection should any unforeseen or unfortunate accident occur, because you took all reasonable steps to mitigate against such situations.

Before Filming

Approximately a week and a half before filming takes place, the opportunity to make last-minute double-checks for all arrangements and bookings should be taken.

Your Producer will take care of this for you, and it will typically involve a telephone call between you to work through the arrangements and establish if anything needs to be double checked.

After the checks have been made, your Producer will report back accordingly.

It may be appropriate and courteous to issue a companywide email notifying staff of filming if it will be carried out at your company's premises.

On The Day of Filming

When it finally comes to it, the day or days of filming are very much enjoyable. It is strongly recommended that as commissioning executive, you attend filming in your capacity as Executive Producer.

It is common for minor questions on set to need answering in an official capacity by your company and you should be readily be able to give these.

Filming days are quite tiring; days are long and breaks are short. It is a production courtesy that as the client you are catered for during lunch and other breaks.

Filming operations also provide an excellent opportunity to gather high quality social media content. If you are able to attend filming, it is worth bringing a stills camera or even a video camera so that you can capture some behind-the-scenes social media content for your company's social and blog post output.

About The Author

James has 17 years' experience in broadcast television and corporate video production. As a specialist in producing videos for business, he draws extensively on his production background as well his expertise as a published marketing consultant.

He is the Director of WOW Video Production, which specialises in providing marketing agencies with a complete video production service that can be fully white labelled, as well as working with individual clients directly.

James' background in direct marketing is key to his ability to ensure that work which he and his team produce communicates in the most effective way possible with the intended target audience. In addition, these videos do so with a particularly high level of comprehension, retention and where appropriate, action on behalf of the viewer.

For any agency partner requests or client enquiries, you can contact James directly: james@wowvideoproduction.co.uk

Company website: www.wowvideoproduction.co.uk

Special Thanks & Mentions

Dave Symondson

John Hoare

Laura Winter

Jeremy Fall

Amy Culora

Paul Baker

Elliot Messenger

Mark Southern

Howard Phillis

Peter Dickson

Mark Evans

Russell Holley

Vicky McDonough

Ben Rush

Lee Peck

Ryan Lisk

Alex Winsor

Nick May

Callum Logan

Amy Sanger

Bevan Wilkinson

Bogdan Popescu

BEHIND THE SCENES PICTURES

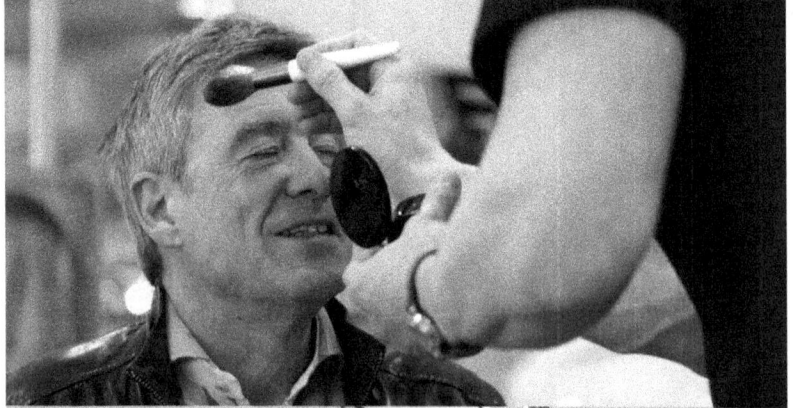

www.ingramcontent.com/pod-product-compliance
Lightning Source LLC
Chambersburg PA
CBHW071114210326
41519CB00020B/6294